# A Moon in Your Lunch Box

# A Moon
# in Your
# Lunch Box

Poems by
MICHAEL SPOONER

Illustrations by
IB OHLSSON

A Redfeather Book
*Henry Holt and Company • New York*

Thanks to these consultants:
Syl, Mark, Morgan, Tait, and Wendy
—M.S.

Text copyright © 1993 by Michael Spooner
Illustrations copyright © 1993 by Ib Ohlsson
All rights reserved, including the right to reproduce
this book or portions thereof in any form.
First edition
Published by Henry Holt and Company, Inc.,
115 West 18th Street, New York, New York 10011.
Published simultaneously in Canada by Fitzhenry & Whiteside Ltd.,
91 Granton Drive, Richmond Hill, Ontario L4B 2N5.

Library of Congress Cataloging-in-Publication Data
Spooner, Michael.
    A moon in your lunch box: poems / by Michael Spooner;
illustrations by Ib Ohlsson.
    (A Redfeather book)
    Summary: A collection of poems celebrating feelings, seasons,
and topics ranging from lunch boxes to the moon.
    ISBN 0-8050-2209-0 (alk. paper)
    1. Children's poetry, American. [1. American poetry.]
I. Ohlsson, Ib, ill. II. Title. III. Series: Redfeather books.
PS3569.P62M66   1993      811'.54—dc20      92-32662

Printed in the United States, bound in Mexico.
on acid-free paper.∞

10 9 8 7 6 5 4 3 2 1

*This book is for Nancy*
*—M.S.*

*. . . and for Gita, too*
*—I.O.*

# Contents

# I

## *Full moon*

O,
the big
round moon
is a hole
in the sky,

and
the day
washes through
like the
morning tide.

When
the earth
is full
and it's time
for night,

then
the day
washes out
to the
other side.

9

# Changes

The earth sheds its winter quilts
and hurries on toward summer,
    as if it, too, is restless
    for the tree house and the bicycle.

The moon looks rounder
than it did last night;
    I think it knows that I am growing too.

The moth and butterfly emerge
from their cocoons, feeling
     how it feels when all your sleeves
     have grown too short again.

Each day my world shows
one more change;
     each day I see another one in me.

The earth rolls out of hibernation.
The moon slips through its phases in the sky.
The butterfly will try its wings today,

     and so will I,
     and so will I.                                    11

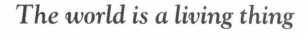

# The world is a living thing

The world is a living thing
    this great wet walloping day.

The wind is a living wind
    that slides up under my arms
    and trots me here and away.

The mud is alive today,
    and its grubby slurping lips
    smooch with the soles of my shoes.

The sky is alive with air
    and the sounds of faraway shouts
    calling me—come and see.

The world is a living thing today.

I'll have to send my face to school,
but my real self is
    rollicking through this
    frolicking through this

walloping springtime day.

# Making faces

don't you know

that if you make
that awful face

  you know the one
  eyelids pulled down
  nose pulled up
  tongue between your fingers—yuck

and if I tiptoe up behind you on my ghost-feet sneakers
    and I

BANG MY LUNCH BAG IN YOUR EAR

hah!
your face is going to stay that way
forever

13

# How the moon gets smaller

Actually, the moon
is nothing but a giant
butter cookie
that gets smaller
bite by bite
because a hungry gang of
rascals nibble at it
night by night.

No one knows exactly who
those nibblers are—
but just between us two,
I wonder why
the second graders
are so sleepy
in the morning,
why they stumble
to their places,

where they got
their cookie breath
and crumbs of mischief
on their faces. . . .

# Mud love

my little bare feet
are cozy in the mud
are crazy for the mud

    my little bare feet
    squirm sweetly in the mud
    and the mud
    grubbies them snugly
    mud gloves

and the mud pretends
to have no shape
my toes pretend
to give it theirs

and the mud pretends
to be the deep round earth
my toes pretend
to be the roots of trees

my little bare feet
are cozy in the mud
are crazy for the mud

my little bare feet
dig deep into the mud
and the mud
snuggles them grubbily
mud love

15

# Neighbors

Somepeople like to
         put up a fence

a hickety rickety white painted pickety
(keep your bikes         on your own side)

                FENCE

to tell the street
                    where the street should be

to tell the neighbors
         that side's you /
                    this side's me.

But I am
      raising a row of sapling green

a ragged row of curving stems
      (of rough sweet bark),
      of vining twines and
      branching tangles,
and oh
the smallest leaves
      greening the sun
           with their little hands

          (and of bright
    busybirds
        neighboring
    cheerily)

tree to tree /
    tree to tree.

# *dragonfly*

*from a line by Louise Bogan*

# Bubble gum

I knew a girl who put
one, two,     three pieces
of bubble         gum in her
mouth and         four, five,
six, pieces         of bubble
gum in         her mouth
and then         she chewed
it seven         days and
blew a         bubble
big as         a house
all pink         and all
leathery         and (this
is true)         that bubble
lifted her like a hot
air balloon
and didn't put
her down till
she got to France.

19

We never saw her again.

# Small miracles

I brought a little telescope
    so we could see the universe of lights;
    they're so bright and so far away, I almost
    think they're pinholes in the night.

    Here, tell me what you see.

I brought a small kaleidoscope
    so we could see the colored snowflakes fly—
    turn it quickly, it's a blizzard; slowly,
    crystal flowers unfolding in your eye.

    Here, tell me what you see.

I brought a poem my friend has written
    so we could see the lazy dance of words,
    the play of rhymes like sunbeams
    on the page; the flight of thoughts like birds.

    Here, tell me what you see.

## Bedtime prayers

Let me close my eyes
    the way a tulip
    folds its petals,
certain that they'll open with the dawn.

Let the window rain
    whisper
    to my dreams;
let my dreams whisper back again.

Let me learn in the dark
    what dark means
    to a little plant—
to its roots—and let me grow.

Let me know, as surely
    as the sun
    goes down,
it's coming up again tomorrow.

21

·II·

# The setting moon

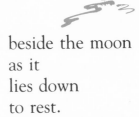

The golden disk
of moon
is sinking
down
and down
and very soon
it's going to land
upon the ocean
like a coin
upon a table,
spinning
round
and round
until it finally
circles down.

And if I had
a sailing boat,
I'd slide away,
I'd glide away
so silently
and fast
that very soon
I'd draw my boat
beside the moon
as it
lies down
to rest.

The golden coin
of moon
afloat
upon the sea
and me,
from my
early-morning
sailboat,
stepping
gently out
upon it.

# The phase I'm going through

I asked my mother
      why the moon is full sometimes
      and dark sometimes and sometimes in between.
She smiled a silly half-moon smile
      and said, "It's all
      a matter of which phase it's in."

I asked my father
      why the baby screams sometimes
      or laughs and wipes his supper in his hair.
He said that children go through phases.
      "Not to worry;
      he'll be through this in a year."

So if I turn my
      dark face to the world sometimes,
      or eat my hat with ketchup and with glue,
or yowl with cats when the moon is full,
      think nothing of it—
      it's just the phase I'm going through.

# How to get there

The highway
runs
from here to there
—no nonsense—
in a line
as quick
and straight
as tools
can make it.

But the river
        paddles side to side,
                visiting all its favorite stops,
            thinking all its favorite thoughts,
        calling on friends,
            playing its games,
                arriving later,
                    but arriving
            all the same.

If I could choose to make
my life
like either one of these,
which, I wonder,
would it be?

25

# *Sightseeing*

I like this

mountain
rising up

above
the car door

into
the window

where I
can see it.

I like its

brown
shoulders,

how the snow
drools down

its chest—
vanilla.

I'll bet
no one

has ever
climbed

that slope
of ice

cream just
to taste it.

Someone should.

26

# In the distance

Out the window of the car,
did you ever see
the yellow moon
far in the distance
moving
as you rode along?

All the buildings,
barns,
fence posts,
phone poles
in between
slipped past
and fast away,

but that moon,
that one friend
going along the hilltop
as if he were
picking berries
when you drove by,
followed—
wanted to catch up
with you.

I wondered
if you knew—
I was that moon.
That moon was me.
And what I wanted
was to say

I'm still here.

You can visit
anytime.

27

# The first mosquito

mosquito
first       of the
the                 year
                    is
                buzzing
                in and
                out          can
                your              you
                    ear.          stand
                                   it,
                                can
                            you
                                let
                                    her
                                        tiptoe cross your hand,
                stick out her pointy
                            tongue and
                                    b
                                    i
                                    t
                                    e
                                    b
                                    i
                                    t
                                    e
                                    b
                                    i
                                    t
                                    e
                                    ?

28

# These footprints I am making

These
footprints

    I am
    making

know that
I am real,

    that I have
    real feet,

that I am
big enough

    to matter.
    And they

will show
whoever

    happens by
    that I

was here
FIRST.

29

# Fourth of July

can the rockets' red glare have

ascended so brightly puffed into marigold blossoms

*

# The package says:

Don't hold fireworks when you
    light them; you'll be
sorry if you do.

Folks will change your name to
    Lefty, stick your
ears back on with glue.

And don't drop them on the
    baby; that's a
very important rule.

She'll just stick them in her
    mouth, you know,
and cover them with drool.

No!

# How things come to be

Riding up a brand-new street,
I like to think that
if it weren't for me,
there wouldn't be anything to see.

There would be no bikes, no houses, trees,
no dogs on porches,
kids on backyard swings,
or old folks raking leaves.

I like to think
that nothing is—
until I see it;
then it starts to be.

But if it's true
that I create
a street by riding through,
it could as well be true for you.

Would you ride down my street sometime?
Would you look at all my things?
My cat, my house, my bike;
would you use my hammock and my swing?

Since nothing is
until we see it,
let's agree: if I see you,
will you see me?

## *I am not contained
between my hat and boots*

The sun is my right eye;
the moon is my left eye.
The pulse of planets is my heartbeat.

My hair is the thick
jungle of the tropics.
My toes dig deep into the earth.

At night
I trace the path of comets
with my yellow crayon,

and my fingers,
when I splash them in the Dipper,
drip with stars.

33

# A moon in your lunch box

There's a moon
in your lunch box—
I'm not kidding.

Someone left it
like an extra cookie
on a plate of sky,
and I
snatched it up
this morning
just for you.

It was cool
to the touch
and slightly rough,
and I put it there
between your apple
and your sandwich,
glowing.

Take a look,
but don't show
the others—

it's a secret moon
inside your lunch box,

and it is
just for you.

# You can't be full moon all the time

The roses in my garden
     bud
and bloom
     and then they
slowly fade.

The maple leaves
     (tiny green fingers)
spread their palms
     one day
wide open,
     then they blush
and drop away.

The moon
     goes through
its phases too:
     first crescent,
golden full,
     again to crescent,
then it disappears awhile.

I think of this
       each time I've been
important
       for too long.

I guess my friends deserve
       their turn
to lead the line.

You can't be
       full moon
all the time.

## I love autumn

when the trees
are releasing
the leaves
in showers
of yellow
and brown,

and the leaves
are swirling
around
and down,

and the wind
is whirling
them off
the ground,

and I try
to stand up
straight
in my place

to feel
the wet kiss
of fall
on my face.

# Tapping on the window

I tap—
the bird takes flight,
frightened by the monster I
must be to eyes like his.

Of course,
you can't expect
a bird to know that I can't
touch him through the glass.

It makes
me wonder, though,
if many of the monsters
I myself might see

are kept—
by something I
don't understand—quite safely
out of reach of me.

39

# Don't kill the bee

Don't smash him,
don't squash him,
don't step on the bee;

he's much more afraid
than you or me.

Just give him
a lift on
a paper—like so—

then open the window
and let him go.

But don't smack him,
don't whack him
with might and with main.

I'm not going to clean up
the bee guts again.

# Columbus Day

Maybe you're asking:
    what about the people
    who were here before Columbus?

You'd be right to ask that.

Maybe you're wondering:
    what happened to those people
    when the Spanish came with sharpened swords
    and flags flapping in the peaceful breeze?

You'd be right to wonder.

Maybe you're thinking:
    it's nice to know the earth is round,
    but I'm not sure the history books
    remember everything.

You're right. You're right.

# Candles

Sometimes I think
　　that autumn is
　　　　the birthday
　　of the year,
for in the country now,
　　on each round
　　　　cake hill,
　　all the candles
start to flare:
　　yellow, orange,
　　　　red, and brown;
　　one by one,
one by one.

When the north
　　wind blows
　　the candles out,
another winter's
　　almost here.

# Halloween

It wasn't the pumpkin moon that scared me, looming orange in the sky; it wasn't the mad laughter behind the trees; it wasn't the skitter of tiny feet or the ominous howl of a hound as I went sneaking by. I'm not afraid of witches—who believes in them? and goblins, ghosts, and trolls aren't real; I've known that since I was ten. I knew all the kids in costume: Felice and Melissa, the vampire witches, Mark the Frankenstein; Jennifer was the dragon girl, and Nancy the Fairy Queen. No, it wasn't what I could hear or see that made me quake in my shoes, but the feeling that something was watching me— I felt that so strongly on Halloween. Did you?

43

# Fall

Do they call it "fall"
    because the leaves all of a day
    drop from their tree wings
    to feather the earth golden?

Or do they call it "fall"
    because the cat—reaching one paw
    cautiously down from the stoop
    to test this earth of new gold—
    is afraid she might?

# First frost

when the cold comes in
        like the snap of a twig
    and the leaves fairly
        jump from the trees
and leaf-damp Nancy
        and apple-cheeked Isaac
    come stamping in
        from trail blazing
        and pioneer days-ing

        and everyone wants to know—
        will it snow?

when the grass grows a crust
        like the crunch of a boot
    and the air is a
        nip in your nose
and icicle Isaac
        and numb-knuckled Nancy
    come crashing in
        from lunar shoes
        and arctic rescues

        and everyone wants to know—
        will it snow?
        will it snow?

# Fly south

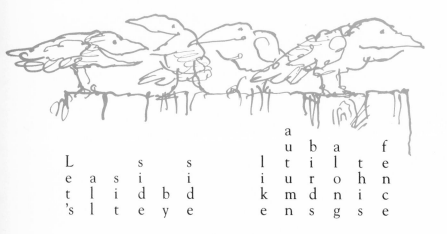

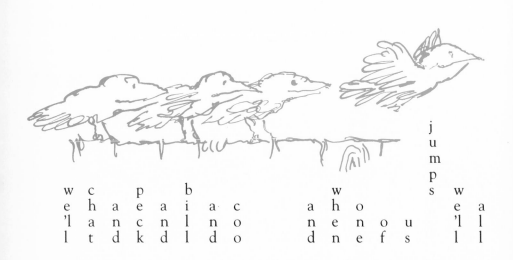

Let's all sit side by side like autumn birds along this fence

we'll chat and peck and bill and coo and when one of us jumps we'll all

```
        ~  ^^    ~   !!    ~~       ~^
     f        s           ^       s  ^
   ^    l     o     ^   f       o  ! )
 (    y      u        l     u        )
 (  ^    ~  f   t        y      t
    ^   ~~  l  ~  h s f  s      h      f
        y         o l  o            l
            s     u  y  u          y
   f ~ !   o f   t          t
     l    u  l h f   s    h        f
     y   t   y   l    o            f l
         h        y   s o u         y
              f        t
              l        h
              y
```

·IV·

# Tonight the moon

Tonight the moon's
  a magic sickle, and
      the man in the
        moon's a bald-head
          farmer reaping heaps
            of stars. Tonight the
              moon's a golden bow
                bent back in goddess
                  hands. Look—just now
                  she sent an arrow
                  stabbing through that
                  dark monster of a cloud.
                  See it flash?   Tonight
                  the moon's a round door
                  opening in the sky, open-
                  ing just a bit, just to let
                  a silver slip of light escape
                  into this world of night.
                  The round-shouldered man
                in the moon stoops down to
              smile out the crescent crack    49
            at you.   Hello.   You look a
        little sad, and I'm just set-
      ting out some tea.   Would you
  care to have a cup with me?

# Walking to school

a

   snow-

      flake

        floating

         playfully

           by,

        stray-fully,

      gay-fully

       dots

       my

       eye ...

# Giant language

If you say a word
  like NO

        as      slooooow    as you can say it
        and in a voice as low as low

NNNNNNNNNNNNOOOOOOOOOO OOOO OOO O

    you see it really isn't NO at all—
(NO is always short and sharp: NO!)
    stretched out like this

      it changes

           to some other word

some word in Giant Language
you are not required to know

        for no one knows
        what Giant Language means—
        I don't, I readily confess—

     and maybe
     (mind you, this is just
     a guess) maybeMAYBE

NNNNNNNNNNNNOOOOOOOOOO OOOO OOO O

       in Giant Language
   is the word for
          YES!

51

# My banana

*(apologies to R.L.S.)*

I have a small banana
    that has come to lunch with me,
but what can be the use of it
    is more than I can see.

I'll mash it and I'll smash it
    and I'll smush it in my cup;
~I'll pour my Pepsi on it,
    and then I'll drink it up.

# Trimming the tree

my
spruce,
my little
evergreen, deep
green, black green:
plumped and decked in snow.
two cardinals,
two scarlet puffs
of warmth, apple red,
cranberry red:    ornaments on
the
bough.

# Christmas morning

This frosted morning,
crisp and clear,

> before the hawk
> begins to stir
> among the branches,

> before the fox
> sets out
> upon her
> hunting rounds;

this early morning,
as the moon looks quietly

> from tips of trees
> on silence that came down
> like cotton
> with the snow,

> and the spruces fluff
> dark feathers
> against the cold;

this hopeful morning,
near the turning of the year,

I send my breath
out in a cloud,
and with it

I send all
the hateful thoughts
I had all year—
and they disperse.

This Christmas morning

I can just imagine
peace on earth.

# Nancy's navel

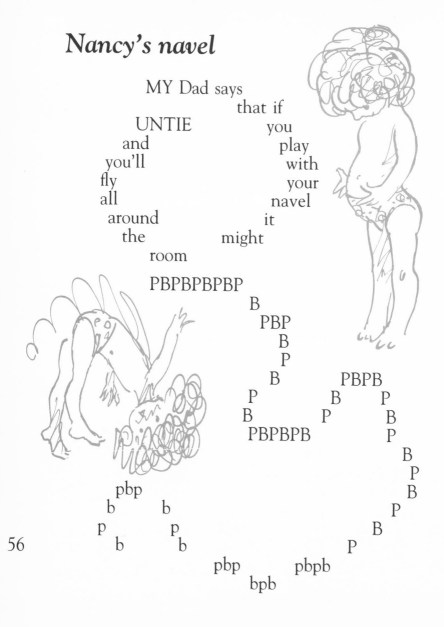

MY Dad says

that if

UNTIE

you

and

play

you'll

with

fly

your

all

navel

around

it

the

might

room

PBPBPBPBP

B

PBP

B

P

B

PBPB

P

B

P

B

P

B

PBPBPB

P

B

P

B

P

B

P

pbp

b

b

p

p

b

b

pbp

pbpb

bpb

like a runaway balloon

   and you'll end up on the bookshelf

or the back of the dresser

   and bedead until morning

# Cat's cradle

Take this loop of string
and slip your hands inside.
Twist your fingers here and here;
now turn your palms away.

Sometimes don't you think
our life is like this—
always turning over,
always changing shape?

Catch this circle with your thumbs,
this one with your little fingers.

It's always twisting funny ways
until we see a pattern for a moment;
until we see a startling design.

Close your hands together now
as if you're going to pray.
Turn them out.   Now open.

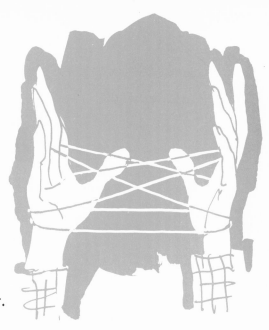

Cat's cradle.
Cup and saucer.
Owl's eyes.

We need some tension on the string,
a little stress to keep
our lines true, the pattern clear.

Soldier's bed.
Apache door.
The butterfly.

I can't wait to see
what shape we'll have next year.

59

# Winter nights

I want to lie down
        where the snow
    is deep,
lie on my back
    where the silence of snow
    is thick,
and where great
        white drifts
        drop into curves
        and hollows
round the bases of trees.

I want to look up
        straight up
    from a bed
in deep snow
    and see the stars
        wheeling round
    as if I lay silently
        over the pin
    that keeps them
stuck to earth.

In my heart
    I feel a secret
    soft and still—
        like
    a winter mouse
        curled up and dozing
        under deep deep snow.
Even I
    am not sure
what my heart's secret is,
        but I know
    it has to do
        with winter,
        with the slow wheeling stars
and the stillness of snow.

## *Winter dreams*

Sleepishly, snoozily
    snug into bed,
I'm dragging the blankets
    up over my head.

Late in the year,
    in the deep of December,
warmly I'm wishing
    a wish for spring.

Creepishly, crawlishly
    cold caterpillar
tugs his cocoon
    over 42 shoulders.

Deep in the year
    in the dark of December,
drowsily dreaming
    a dream of wings.

# Close this book

Enough—
    no more frippery.
Poetry's
    for naughty, idle
children
    who have nothing else to do.
and you,
    my friend, are not that sort.
HOMEWORK
    is for you.

Close
    this book, I said,
and hide
    it on a shelf.
If you
    read it very often,
I'm afraid,
    you might begin to write such
silliness
    yourself.